Pets in my house

Cats

Jennifer Blizin Gillis

Raintree

www.raintreepublishers.co.uk
Visit our website to find out more information about **Raintree** books.

To order:
☎ Phone 44 (0) 1865 888112
▤ Send a fax to 44 (0) 1865 314091
▣ Visit the Raintree Bookshop at **www.raintreepublishers.co.uk** to browse our catalogue and order online.

First published in Great Britain by Raintree, Halley Court, Jordan Hill, Oxford OX2 8EJ, part of Harcourt Education.
Raintree is a registered trademark of Harcourt Education Ltd.

Editorial: Catherine Clarke and Daniel Cuttell
Design: Michelle Lisseter
Picture Research: Jill Birschbach and Maria Joannou
Production: Amanda Meaden

Originated by Dot Gradations Ltd
Printed and bound in Hong Kong, China by South China Printing Company

ISBN 1 844 43571 7
09 08 07 06 05
10 9 8 7 6 5 4 3 2 1

British Library Cataloguing in Publication Data
Blizin Gillis, Jennifer
Cats. – (Pets in my house)
636.8
A full catalogue record for this book is available from the British Library.

Acknowledgements
The publishers would like to thank the following for permission to reproduce photographs: Animals Animals p.**18** (Renee Stockdale); Dwight Kuhn pp.**6**, **8**, **23(d)**; Getty Images p.**7** (top) (Digital Vision); Harcourt Education Ltd pp.**4** (Greg Williams), **5** (Jill Birschbach), **14** (Greg Williams), **15** (Greg Williams), **16** (Greg Williams), **17** (Greg Williams), **19** (Dave Bradford), **22** (Dave Bradford), **23(a)** (Dave Bradford), **23(b)** (Greg Williams), **23(c)** (Greg Williams), **23(e)** (Greg Williams), back cover (Greg Williams); Scott Braut pp.**7** (bottom), **10**, **11**, **12**, **13**, **20**, **21**; Tudor Photography p.**9**.

Cover photograph reproduced with permission of Scott Braut.

The publishers would like to thank Michaela Miller for her assistance in the preparation of this book.

Every effort has been made to contact copyright holders of any material reproduced in this book. Any omissions will be rectified in subsequent printings if notice is given to the publishers.

The paper used to print this book comes from sustainable resources.

Contents

Some words are shown in bold, **like this**.
You can find them in the glossary on page 23.

What kind of pet is this?

Pets are animals that live with us.

Some pets are small and slippery.

My pet is small and furry.

Can you guess what kind of pet this is?

What are cats?

Cats are **mammals**.

Mammals make milk for their babies.

There are big cats in the wild.

Pet cats are small and live in houses with people.

Where did my cat come from?

A mother cat had a litter of kittens.

At first, the kittens could not see.

They stayed with their mother for ten weeks.

Then, I took one of the kittens home.

How big is my cat?

At first, my kitten was as small as your hand.

It weighed as much as a very small bag of sugar.

Now my kitten is a grown up cat.

It is about as big as a pair of adult's shoes.

Where does my cat live?

My cat lives in the house with us.

It does not need a special house.

My cat has a bed.

It is soft and round.

What does my cat eat?

My cat eats special cat food.

Sometimes it eats cooked fish, too.

I always give my cat water
to drink.

Sometimes I give it treats.

What else does my cat need?

When it is inside the house, my cat needs a **litter tray**.

It is like a cat toilet.

My cat needs a **collar** with a name tag.

This can help me find my cat if it gets lost.

What can I do for my cat?

I play with my cat every day.

Playing is good exercise for cats.

I brush my cat every week.

Brushing keeps my cat's **coat** shiny.

What can my cat do?

My cat is strong.

It can jump high.

My cat is clever.

It knows how to open doors!

Cat map

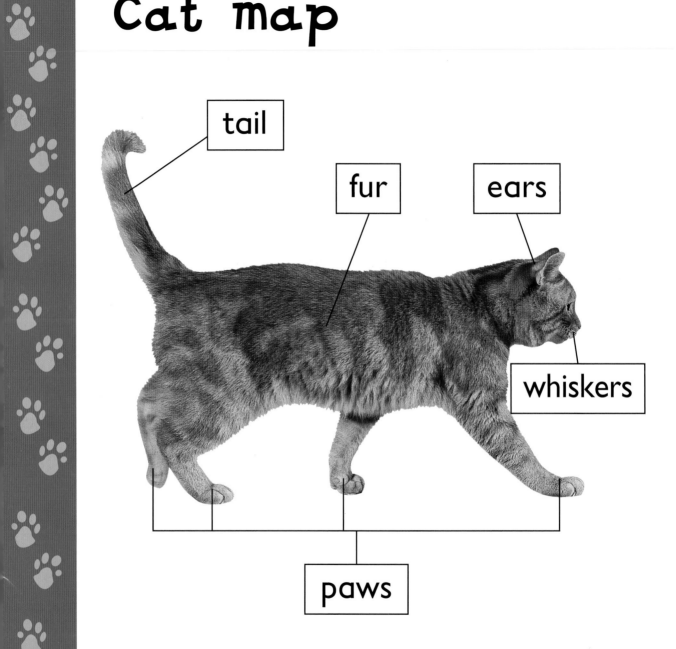

tail

fur

ears

whiskers

paws

Glossary

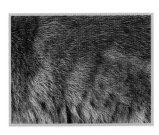

coat
thick hair or fur that covers an animal's body

collar
cloth or leather band a pet wears around its neck

litter tray
small tray cats use as a toilet

mammal
animal that has hair or fur and that makes milk for its babies

Index

Titles in the *Pets In My House* series include:

Hardback   1 844 43570 9

Hardback   1 844 43571 7

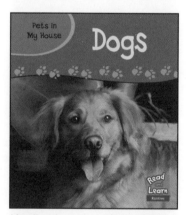

Hardback   1 844 43572 5

Hardback   1 844 43573 3

Hardback   1 844 43574 1

Find out about the other titles in this series on our website www.raintreepublishers.co.uk